What Can I Be?

I Can Be Anything

MAURICE E. JONES, FMP

A Book to Inspire All Children

Tellwell Talent
www.tellwell.ca

ISBN
978-0-2288-9627-2 (Hardcover)
978-0-2288-9626-5 (Paperback)

POSITIVE ATTITUDE

POSITIVE ENERGY

POSITIVE RESULTS

TABLE OF CONTENTS

ACKNOWLEDGMENTS

<u>My Creator</u>

<u>My Mom:</u>
Mrs. Nancy J. Jones, who sat me down to read and write every day, and who still inspires me

<u>My Son:</u>
Mr. Maurice, who still teaches me something new all the time

<u>My Teachers:</u>
My teachers, who left a lasting impression on me

Mrs. Jackson — Sanders Elementary
Mr. Hudson — Herman Elementary
Mrs. Moore — Herman Elementary
Mr. Little — Lessenger Middle School
Mrs. Brown — Drew Middle School
Mrs. Hanna — Mackenzie High School
Mr. Walker — Mackenzie High School
Mrs. Harris — Mackenzie High School
Mrs. McCuin — Murray-Wright High School
Mrs. Taylor — Murray-Wright High School
Mrs. Cannon — Murray-Wright High School

Thank you for teaching me and believing in me.

Maurice E. Jones, FMP
"MW81"

DEDICATION

This book is dedicated to all the teachers who have been there for their students; who have paid for supplies out of their own pockets; who come to work every day, sometimes under harsh conditions; who are willing to talk to us; who are willing to listen to us; who teach until we understand; who show that they truly care; who encourage us; who help prepare us for the world.

From our A, B, Cs to English and geometry, you are truly the backbone of our educational journey. Your nurturing, love, support, passion, and dedication are unmatched. You are truly remarkable. Thank you for all that you do.

Sincerely,

Maurice Edward Jones, FMP

Detroit Public School Alumni K-12

Murray-Wright H.S. "81"

WHAT CAN 1  ?

AMAZING!

by

Maurice E. Jones, FMP

I can be

an
Astronaut —

so that I can travel into space

a
Baseball player —

so that I can help my
team achieve victory

I can be

a
Chef—
so that I can make great
food for people

a
Doctor—
so that I can help make
people feel better

I can be

an
Engineer —
so that I can construct buildings

a
Firefighter —
so that I can put out
fires and save lives

I can be

a

General—

so that I can lead my
troops in battle

a

Hockey player—

so that I can use my skills on ice

I can be

an
Inventor —

so that I can create
great opportunities

a
Judge —

so that I can make sure that
we all are treated fairly

I can be

a

Keyboardist —

so that I can make great music

a

Lawyer —

so that I can stand up for justice

I can be

a

Mathematician —

so that I can solve problems

a

Nurse —

so that I can help sick
people get better

I can be

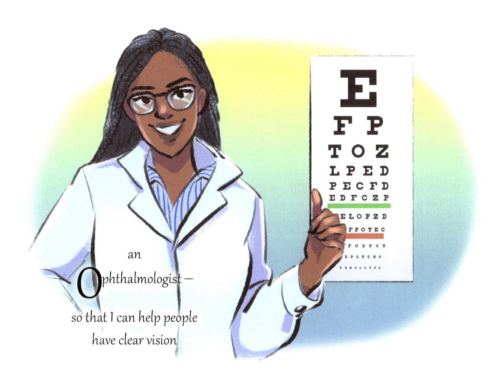

an

Ophthalmologist —

so that I can help people
have clear vision

a

Poet —

so that I can share
beautiful thoughts

I can be

a
Quarterback —

so that I can lead my team to win

a
Reporter —

so that I can report good news

I can be

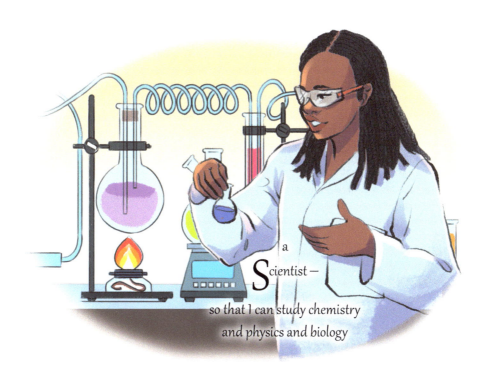

a
Scientist —

so that I can study chemistry
and physics and biology

a
Teacher —

so that I can give you knowledge
to be a future leader

I can be

a
Urologist —
so that I can diagnose
and treat diseases

a
Violinist —
so that I can make
soothing sounds

I can be

a **W**riter —

so that I can share positive experiences

an **X**-ray technician —

so that I can see inside
you to help you

I can be

a
Yoga instructor—

so that I can help keep
you in shape

a
Zoologist—

so that I can help
the animals

INDEX

Notable Achievements of Black Americans

ASTRONAUT:

Bluford, Guion Stewart, Jr — The first Black American in space aboard the Space Shuttle Challenger in 1983

Jemison, Mae Carol — The first Black American female in space aboard the Space Shuttle Endeavour in 1992

Wilson, Stephanie — The first Black American to fly three missions in space and most days in space, totaling forty-two as of 2021

BASEBALL PLAYER:

Aaron, Henry — Retired as the all-time leader in home runs in 1976; Elected to Hall of Fame in 1982

Flood, Curt — The first to fight for free agency in sports, 1969

Robinson, Jackie — The first Black American in baseball in modern era, 1947; Analyst, 1965; Executive V.P., 1957

Walker, Moses Fleetwood — The first Black American to play major league baseball in 1884 for Toledo Blue Stockings

---

CHEF:

Evans, Darryl — The first Black American to compete in the International Culinary Olympics, winning three gold medals in 1988

Lee, Robert W — The first Black American executive chef at Harrisburg Hotel, PA; Chef of the Year, 1970–1979

Russell, Mariya — The first Black American female to win a Michelin Star, 2019

West, Leon — Awarded Chef of the Year by the Culinary Federation, 1996; Culinary Hall of Fame, Heritage Foundation, 1997

DOCTOR:

Canady, Alexa Irene	The first Black American neurosurgeon, 1981; Michigan Hall of Fame, 1989
Dickens, Helen Octavia	The first Black American Director of Obstetrics and Gynecology; Mercy-Douglass Hospital, 1948
Drew, Charles Richard	The first Black American to serve as Examiner on Board of Surgeons, 1941; Created the blood bank
Williams, Daniel Hale	Performed the first successful open-heart surgery in 1893 at Chicago Provident Hospital

ENGINEER:

Exline, Brittney	The youngest Black female to become an engineer in the United States at age nineteen, 2011
Grant, Howard P	The first Black graduate from University of California, Berkeley in Civil Engineering, 1948
Jackson, Mary	The first Black female engineer for NASA, 1958

FIREFIGHTER:

Hatton, Earl L	The first Black firefighter promoted to Fire Investigation Unit in St. Louis, 1952
Taylor, Marcena	The first Black firefighter, 1938; The first captain, 1952; The first battalion chief, 1969, Detroit, Michigan
Williams, Molly	The first Black female firefighter in U.S. history, 1818

GENERAL:

Anderson, Marcia	The first Black female as Major General in the U.S. Army and U.S. National Guard, 2011
Davis, Benjamin O. Sr	The first Black American to rank Brigadier General of the U.S. Army, 1940
Harris, Marcelite J	The first Black American female Major General in the U.S. Air Force, 1995
Powel, Colin Luther	The first Afro-Caribbean American as Chairman of the Joint Chiefs of Staff, 1989

HOCKEY:

Fuhr, Grant Scott	The first Black player to win the Stanley Cup, 1984; Inducted into the Hockey Hall of Fame, 2003
Grier, Michael James	The first Black person to be a General Manager in league history, 2022
James, Angela Diane	The first Black female player to be inducted into the Hall of Fame, 2010
O'Ree, William Eldon	The first Black player in the history of the National Hockey League, 1958; Inducted into the Hall of Fame, 2018

INVENTOR:

Croak, Marian	Invented Voice over Internet Protocol; Inducted into the National Inventors Hall of Fame, 2022; 200 patents
Lawson, Gerald	Designed the Fairchild Channel F video console and video game cartridge
Moss, Leo	The first known Black dollmaker in U.S., late 1800s
Jones, Fredrick McKinley	The first Black member in the Society of Refrigeration Engineers, 1944; National Medal of Technology, 1991; Sixty-one patents

JUDGE:

Jackson, Ketanji Brown	The first Black female Supreme Court Justice in the U.S., 2022
Marshall, Thurgood	The first Black Supreme Court Justice in the United States, 1967
McCree, Wade H. Jr	The first Black American appointed U.S. Circuit Judge of U.S. Court of Appeals, Sixth Circuit, 1966
Motley, Constance Baker	The first Black woman to argue at the Supreme Court; The first Federal Judiciary U.S. District Judge in New York, 1966

KEYBOARDIST:

Hancock, Herbie	Classically trained at age seven; Kennedy Center Award, 2013; Academy Award, 1986
Keys, Alicia	Classically trained pianist, composing songs at age twelve; Signed with Columbia Records at age fifteen
Wonder, Stevie	Blind shortly after birth; Signed with Motown at age eleven; Awarded the Presidential Medal of Freedom in 2014

LAWYER:

Archer, Dennis — Served as first Black President of the American Bar Association, 2002

Hooks, Benjamin — Awarded the Spingarn Medal from NAACP, 1986; Awarded the Presidential Medal of Freedom, 2007

Ray, Charlotte E — The first Black Female Lawyer in U.S.; admitted to the District of Columbia Bar, 1872

MATHEMATICIAN:

Blackwell, David — The first Black American to be inducted into National Academy of Sciences, 1965

Cox, Elbert Frank — The first Black person in history to receive a PhD in Mathematics, 1925, Cornell University

Haynes, Euphemia — The first Black woman with a PhD in Mathematics, Catholic University of America, 1943; Chair, DC Board of Education, 1966

Johnson, Katherine — Developed calculations to launch astronauts to space and the moon, 1961–1969; Awarded the Medal of Freedom, 2015

Vaughan, Dorothy — The first Black woman supervisor at NASA; FORTRAN expert; Awarded the Congressional Gold Medal in 2019

NURSE:

Mahoney, Mary Eliza — The first Black American registered nurse in U.S., 1879; inducted into the American Nurses Hall of Fame, 1976

Washington, Col. Lawrence — The first male nurse and Black male nurse to ever serve in the U.S. Army, 1967

Williams, Betty Smith — The first Black nurse graduate, Case Western Reserve University, 1954; Co-founder of NBNA, 1971

OPHTHALMOLOGY:

Bath, Patricia — The first Black American Resident in Ophthalmology, NYU; Holder of five patents

Fountain, Tamara — The first Black Woman to be named President of the American Academy of Ophthalmology, 2021

McDonough, Donald K — The first Black American eye specialist in the U.S.; The first Black graduate from Lafayette College, 1844

POET:

Bontemps, Arna	Earned two Guggenheim Fellowships
Brooks, Gwendolyn	The first Black American to win the Pulitzer Prize in Poetry, 1950; The first Black woman at the Academy of Arts and Letters
Gorman, Amanda S.C	National Youth Poet Laureate, 2017; Recited at the Inauguration of U.S. President Joe Biden, 2021
Hayden, Robert	The first Black American Consultant in Poetry to the Library of Congress,1976–78; Academy of Poets, 1975
Wheatley, Phyllis	The first Black American author of a published book of poetry, Poems on Various Subjects, Religious and Moral, 1773

QUARTERBACK:

Briscoe, Marlin	The first Black starting quarterback in NFL history, 1968; College Hall of Fame, 2016
Moon, Warren	Undrafted, first and only Black Hall of Fame Quarterback in NFL, 2006; Canadian football, 2001
Williams, Doug	The first Black starting quarterback to win the Super Bowl, 1988; co-founder of the Black College Football Hall of Fame

REPORTER:

Bradley, Ed	The first Black White House correspondent for CBS News, 1976; Twenty-times Emmy Awards winner
Haynes, Trudy	The first Black TV weather reporter in U.S., Detroit, 1963; The first Black reporter in Philadelphia, 1965
Simpson, Carole	The first Black woman to anchor a major U.S. newscast; Awarded Journalist of the Year, 1992
Dunnigan, Alice	The first Black female correspondent in U.S., 1948; Inducted into the Black Journalist Hall of Fame, 1985

SCIENTIST:

Daly, Marie Maynard	*The first Black woman with a PhD, Columbia University; the first Black woman with a PhD in chemistry in the U.S.,* 1947
Jackson, Shirley	*The first Black woman with a doctorate, MIT,* 1973; *Awarded the National Medal of Science,* 2014
Parker, Carolyn	*Master's degree in physics from Massachusetts Institute of Technology (MIT),* 1951; *The first Black woman known to have a postgraduate degree in physics,* MIT, 1952-1953
Young, James Edward	*The first Black tenure of Physics, MIT,* 1969; *Founding member of the National Society of Black Physicists,* 1977

TEACHER:

Bethune, Mary McLeod	*Founded the National Council of Negro Women,* 1935, *Merged Bethune-Cookman University*
Huston, Gordon David	*The first Black American from Cambridge to graduate from Harvard University,* 1904
Slowe, Lucy Diggs	*The first Dean of Women at any university in U.S. history; The first Black tennis champion,* 1917; *Founder of Alpha Kappa Alpha, the first sorority founded by African American women at Howard University,* 1908
Walker, John	*My high school academic teacher who was very influential in my growth and knowledge,* 1977–1980
Woodson, Carter G	*Pioneer of Black History Month,* 1926; *Dean of Howard & W. Virginia St.; University of Harvard PhD,* 1912

UROLOGIST

Bennett, Carol Joan	*The first Black woman to be board-certified by the American Board of Urology,* 1987
Hawkins, Bobbilynn	*The first Black American full professor of urology; The first female urologist in the United States Army*
Jones, R. Frank	*The first Black diplomat; American Board of Urology,* 1936

VIOLINIST:

Briggs, Karen	Playing professionally at age fifteen; Virginia Symphony Orchestra, 1983; JFK Center for the Performing Arts, 2001, 2004, and 2007
Carter, Regina	Legendary violinist from Detroit Michigan, studying violin since age four; MacArthur Fellows Program, 2006
Davis, Daniel	Juilliard School of Music, 2005; Apollo Award, 2007; Performed for Presidential Candidate Barack Obama, 2007
Dworkin, Aaron Paul	Masters in Violin Performance, 1998; founder of Sphinx Organization, 1996; MacArthur Fellows Program, 2005

WRITER:

Angelou, Maya	Spingarn Medal, 1994; National Medal of Arts, 2000; Presidential Medal of Freedom, 2011
Brown, Jericho	American Book Award Winner for Please, 2009; Pulitzer Prize Winner in Poetry for The Tradition, 2020
Haley, Alex	Pulitzer Prize for novel Roots, 1977; Spingarn Medal, 1977
Wright, Richard	The first Black American Author-Book-of-the-Month, Native Son, 1940; Guggenheim Fellowship, 1939; Spingarn Medal, 1941
Morrison, Toni	American Book Award winner for Beloved and Pulitzer Prize winner for Fiction for Beloved, 1988; Nobel Prize for Literature, 1993
Walker, Alice	National Book Award; Pulitzer Prize Winner; Black Woman for Fiction, The Color Purple; 1983

X-RAY TECHNICIAN:

Allen Jr., William E	The first Black certified X-ray technician; The first Black American College of Radiology Member and Fellow; 1949
Logan, Myra Adele	Elected as a Fellow of the American College of Surgeons, 1951; The first African American woman to perform a successful open-heart surgery, 1943, Harlem Hospital
Webb MD, Dr. Jennifer	The first African American in Michigan to pass the National American Board of Radiology exam; Board-certified radiation oncologist

YOGA INSTRUCTOR:

Bondy, Dianne	Leader of the Yoga for All movement; International best-selling author of Yoga for Everyone
Evans, Dr. Stephanie Y	Author of Black Women's Yoga History: Memoirs of Inner Peace; PhD in Afro-American Studies, 2003
Lawrence, Elvrid	Founder and Executive Director of Institute of Kemetic Yoga in the United States
Trahan, Kerrie	Owner and Founder of Yoganic Flow in Detroit, Michigan

ZOOLOGIST:

Allen, Tanesha	Master's degree from Cambridge and PhD from Oxford University
Turner, Charles Henry	First Black American with a graduate degree, University of Cincinnati, 1891; PhD, University of Chicago, 1907
Young, Roger Arliner	The first Black woman with a Doctorate in Zoology, 1940
Just, Ernest E	Head of Zoology, Howard University, 1912; Co-founder of Omega Psi Phi-Howard University, 1911

You can be all of these things and more but what's most important is that you be yourself.

I CAN BE

For what do you yearn?
Listen to your teacher, and you will learn.

Work hard in school.
Don't be a fool; follow the rules.

Pay attention in class; don't be shy.
With love and guidance, you will reach the sky.

You can be whatever you want to be.
Just keep dreaming; this you'll see.

A Poem for You

Written by
M. Edward Jones, FMP

ENCOURAGEMENT

Keep dreaming

cause

You are Amazing!

DID YOU KNOW?

BLACK INVENTORS

INVENTOR:	PRODUCT:	DATE:
Alexander, Nathaniel	Folding Chair	1911
Boone, Sarah	Ironing Board	1887
Banneker, Benjamin	Almanac	1791
Cherry, Matthew A.	Tricycle	1886
Dorsey, Osbourn	Doorknob	1878
Downing, Paul L.	Mailbox	1891
Elkins, Thomas	Chamber Commode	1897
Fleming Jr., Robert F.	Guitar	1886
Grant, George T.	Golf Tee	1899
Jones, Frederick M.	Air Conditioning Unit	1949
Latimer, Lewis	Electric Lamb Bulb	1882
Love, John L.	Pencil Sharpener	1897
Martin, Washington A.	Lock	1893
Miles, Alexander	Elevator	1867
Morgan, Garrett	Traffic Light	1923
Newman, Lydia O.	Hairbrush	1898
Richardson, William H.	Baby Buggy	1889
Sampson, George T.	Clothes Dryer	1971
Smith, John H.	Lawn Sprinkler	1897
Winters, Joseph W.	Fire Escape Ladder	1878

Know Your History!

WHAT ARE YOU DREAMING ABOUT? WRITE YOUR DREAM DOWN AND VISUALIZE IT!

ABOUT THE AUTHOR

Mr. Maurice E. Jones is a certified chef, poet, and writer, born and raised in Detroit, Michigan by a single parent. He is a product of the Detroit Public School system. His mother inspired him to become a Chef. He has been recognized for his cooking, leadership, and mentoring throughout his culinary career.

He started writing poetry as a teenager followed by short stories, and children's stories after high school. His poem "Gratitude" was published in Collected Whispers by the International Library of Poetry and he was recognized for Outstanding Achievement in Poetry in 2008.

Maurice supports the Children's Hospital of Michigan, HUB-Horizons Upward Bound, VA Hospital of Michigan, Susan B. Komen Breast Cancer Awareness, St. Jude Children's Research Hospital, and several other causes.

Maurice is also a member of the Charles H. Wright Museum of African American History and the Greater St. Mark Baptist Church in Detroit, Michigan.

Always Remember:
Positive Attitude / Positive Energy / Positive Results

Printed in the USA
CPSIA information can be obtained
at www.ICGtesting.com
JSHW042045210624
65084JS00001B/3